AF440978

Yosemite Dawning

Poems of The Sierra Nevada

Shauna Potocky

Cirque Press

Published by
Cirque Press

Sandra Kleven — Michael Burwell
3157 Bettles Bay Loop
Anchorage, AK 99515

Print ISBN: 979-888895315-0

Library of Congress Control Number

cirquejournal@gmail.com
www.cirquejournal.com

Front Cover art "Seeing is Believing" by Penny Otwell

Ending Page art "Rock Sanctuary" by Penny Otwell

Artist Photo by Richard Beebe

Author Photo (About the Author) by Kirk Keeler

Author Photo (back cover) by Colby Brokvist

Interior Illustrations and Paintings: "El Capitan Night Sky", "Taft Point and Cathedral Spires", "Eastern Sierra in Fall" by Shauna Potocky

Book Design by Signe Nichols

Map by Shauna Potocky

Offer the best of yourself
to the world
as faulty as your best
might be.

Go, try
again and again
to bring lightness
to the long, tiring day.

"At the heart of my emerging voice was the belief
that nature held the secret to harmony and unity,
not just outside us, but inside us, no separation."

Terry Tempest Williams
From *When Women Were Birds*

"Look at the rock a different way."

Janet Johnson, climbing partner
Cathedral Peak, August 2005

To Pat,

Life gave us trails that even separated by miles and miles
never made us distant.
Thank you for the love, friendship, care and years.

To Roubaix "Roo",

The truest love I've known.

OREGON
N
CALIFORNIA
Lake Tahoe
CASCADE RANGE
Sacramento
SIERRA NEVADA
YOSEMITE NATIONAL PARK
Mono Lake
COASTAL
San Francisco
Santa Cruz
Mariposa
Lee Vining
SIERRA NATIONAL FOREST
GREAT
RANGES
(CENTRAL) VALLEY
Merced
June Lake
Oakhurst
NEVADA
Fresno
PACIFIC OCEAN
MOJAVE DESERT
Los Angeles
CHANNEL ISLANDS
San Diego

The poems within this book reflect connections to the land, its processes and inhabitants stretching from the Central Valley of California, through the foothhills and forests, into the reaches of the high country of Yosemite, and to the Eastside of the Sierra.

These lands are the traditional homelands of American Indians, people who have been here since time immemorial. Their deep knowledge, culture and care stewarded the land before us.

Their stewardship to these places continues today. I honor and respectfully acknowledge their connection and care of these landscapes and the spirit and processes within.

Dear Reader, if you are unfamiliar with the people and tribes of California, their homelands, languages, deep knowledge, steward-ship, culture and arts, I encourage you to learn more.

Table of Contents

Inheritance

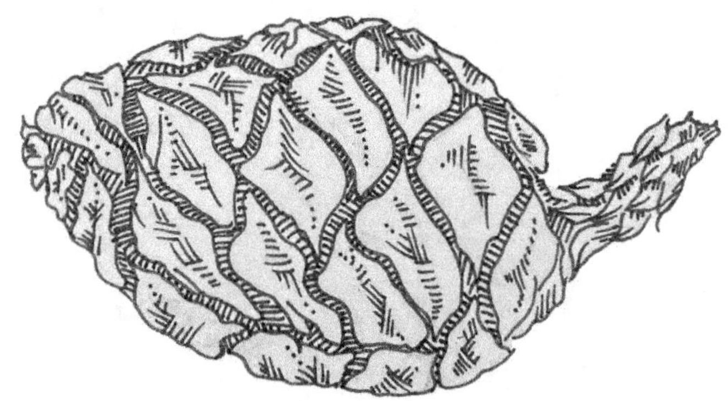

You and I
travel through canyons
you sing prayer songs
among hidden graves

Who knows
how many elders, children
did not make it
the anguish of the ambush.

Your basket carries promises
stones, seeds, secrets
purges and offerings
turned ash in the sweat house.

Beyond this
and the wind
it is not
my story to tell.

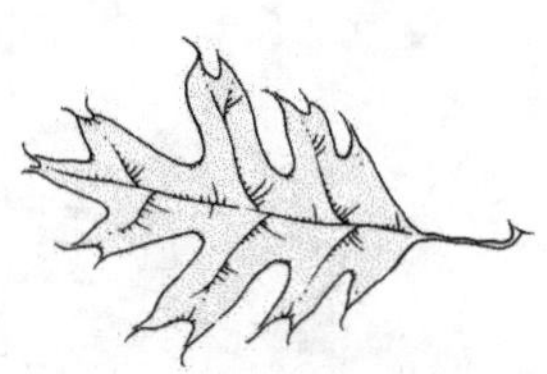

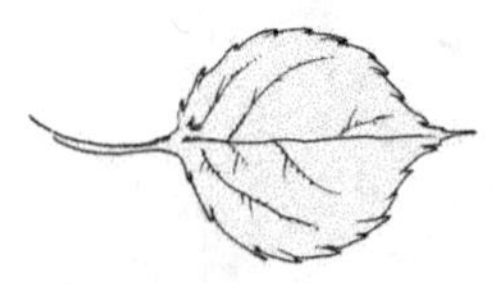

GALEN: CALM AMIDST CLAMORING

You came like so many would
to heal

Your lungs in the true air
settle the mind
after struggle

Turning egg sized Sequoia cones
over in your hands
tiny seeds shook out

Rooted something different
seed bed sparking
something new

Proving
to care, dare for what is novel
has the power to change everything

So Signed, Lincoln

When the ink first touched the page
its wet pigment filling the paper's pores,
No one could have known.

Sweeping up the A, slight curl at the edge
like a leaf dried or flower unfurling,
No one could have known.

While the country endeavored to spill its own blood
what feelings toiled; what hope was budding
as the A turned into a name.

That far off, home to some, unseen by most
the granite stood as nature's beacon
the water falling, its roar uplifting human hope

Its quiet forests filled with giants
whose crowns wide and reaching
touch clouds, clear skies, starry nights

Where in the voice of mountain streams
and rustling leaves, shy footsteps of all
the Sierra's creatures are found to walk

No one could have known.

That as the loop of the L was made
in the wake of dispossession, recognition
and pressures yet to come

a line______________________________
to hold plat and progress at the gate.

The I, was not an I for me, but a transformation to the "we"
the N, hard reach and sway of switchbacks yet ahead
the C, a carve of glacial ice, the bend where frigid waters run

The O, a coming out of shadowed past
the L, to learn, to love, to ascend to something higher
the final N, the return from our hard, hard path, kinder.

That last letter penned
certified,
signed, *Secretary*

its trailing ink like the long miles of our collective journey
Yosemite was protected.

As that dark ink stained the page

It heralded something new
to protect, endeavor to be for all
the best of this world's gifts

Tangible and otherwise, spirit lifting
among trees, reach of desert sands,
water catching light, bird song rising

To steward them
from generation to generation
hand-held gifts gently passed on;

The hardest work ahead
protecting them
against the coming ages.

There are few moments,
few stories in which we can reflect
where in hindsight we know the world was changed

As Lincoln blew his breath
across the wet ink
put his pen to rest in its ink well

Do you wonder if he knew,
could have felt
the trajectory of the world had just moved?

Yosemite would lead
inspiring a world to save more
preserve more, steward more into the future.

That in the altruistic understanding, that the world
belongs to all of us, its greatest gifts our collective work,
he must have felt it, in his core, that the world had moved.

With its imperfections
roils which lay ahead
soon enough, refuge for the future

Lands to heal
blood and bonds, war weary,
broken spirits, fevered bodies, fevered Earth

In meadows where ash and sawdust,
turn to soil, lilies rise—
while wetlands cool our edgy fevers

Nib edge, stutter across the grain
his pen marked time
though his eyes would never see it

He must have known.

Ink dried, the signed pages whisked away
through the halls of a busy government, those hurried steps
began the journey, crossing the great threshold—

From present into the future. The best and hardest work ahead
to set aside, to cradle, and gift again and again
the best of all the world to the kin still yet to come.

No one could have known.

Through foresight as well as consequence
though perhaps, just maybe
Lincoln did.

SETTLING THE SIERRA
   —Reflections on mapping, Muir and lore.

While you rambled
what voices did you hush?

Across whose homelands
did you scribe new stories?

On every peak
you claimed for the new world
recorded as a first ascent

In whose foot strikes, handholds
did you follow?

And how, in our own lives
have we been blind to see
and followed suit?

NELDER GROVE: THE TAKING OF TREES

There are stories
in this place
moldering

with the old cabins
turned humus;
moss growing

inside furrowed bark
in the holes that held planks
that balanced men

raking saw blade teeth
through the biggest trees
turned to wide, tall stumps.

Some crosswise things
happened in this place.

This is no lesser grove,
its giants against stumps
its juxtaposition

of progress and preservation
of what seemed gained
against what was lost.

"Prized lumber"
turned splintered ruin
in "frontier" day sepia photos

that today
we shake our heads at.

This is the best place
to tell the story of what was coming
up the western slope.

MILL ON LEWIS CREEK

The vultures are on the threshold
in the dormant black oaks
that reach across this long-forgotten road;
the wood burner from the old mill that stands,
is silent, alone, wearing storms and hot days
on its rusty skin. An overgrown monument;
its heyday long lost to a century of years,
Depression and trees too hard to reach.

This road, pounded by mule hoof
donkey engine, narrow gauge
heaved wood from the steep slopes;
this mill, its gears turned
by the rush of water from Lewis Creek,
and the flume once a wonder
sliding logs for miles, now sits in pieces;
will never be rejoined.

So many trees, their story
ended in board feet and sawdust
on this ground.

Today, the spirit of that
growing West is gone, lost
to the wind, the years,
the graveyards of tombstones
and stumps.

The mighty oaks,
who dared to take root,
now manage the place.
The mill, an apparition, surrounded
on all sides by forest;
its gears long hushed
and only the creek
sings loudly—or laughs.

CADENCE OF THE CREEK

Dry Buckeye leaves orange as brass keep cadence
with the afternoon's light wind, with the tired creek, left lonesome
when the gold pans stayed empty.

Beyond the chatter call of Acorn Woodpeckers
the rapturous drop of White Oak acorns, slender
nut skins dark as chocolate, falling, heavy as stones

forsaken in heat
or foretelling a wet winter.

Beyond the stiff straw yellow grass
there is a pocket of life hiding out:
silver coils of light give away the water

where a raft of ducks sly
beneath the shade of oaks and bay
beyond the recoil of fierce summer light.

The same light
that is turning the California forest to desert.

As the light goes
up comes the song of tiny crickets
singing their presence across the western slope.

How was their chorus in the warm air
the river rhythm and the chatter of birds
not gold enough?

Looking Beyond Us

It is the granite that will remain
those smooth and weathered peaks
that rise through the trees
or pull themselves up
toward the starry night
and weather kissed skies.

It will be the granite
tombstones on parched landscape
void of trees killed by beetles
ravaged by fire
void of river song
and snow storm.

It will be the granite
children climb to look out
on the valleys and canyons, to strain
their eyes across the distances,
looking for the edge, the end
or the bend of the Earth.

It will be here
with all of the parched
and eroded stories before them,
that they will see, that we
the generation of now
did not do enough.

EDGE OF THE REFUGE

Held down all night
the Tule fog breaks as the dawn does;
rises, ethereal, masks the sun's luminance.
Beneath this low cloud, living things stir
water moves, ripples—and the calls come.

In the rise, wings *spread, everything*
outstretches, lifts in the coming light.
Song, chatter, foreign languages of the past
stir the damp cold of morning, each thing
shattering in the waking of day.

The genes of wildness and knowing pass through the generations;
they face boldly, calmly, the hunts, migrations, births, deaths
and this morning, all who wake, have triumphed.
They gather, breed, sing, sigh, continue the journey
their breathy words rise, sink, fade...

Their final syllables muffled as they come to rest
at the edges of the wetland, dampened by the wild
songs of the redwing black birds, who hold the line
in the tall, wind chilled icy reeds
that hold back the hunters and the rest of us.

Navigating the Crux

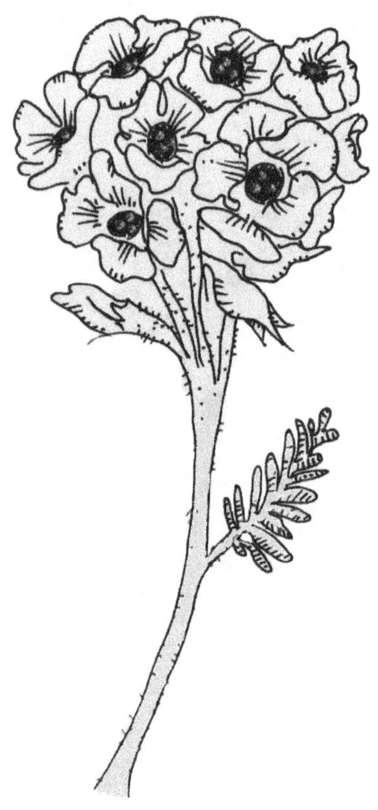

Sky Pilots of Mount Dana

Aren't our lives
like the Sky Pilot
rare, connected, short

Our brilliance, ephemeral
like wild flowering
on one good day of bloom?

OFF-ROUTE
   —For J.M. and your *wild life* loving heart.

When you fell
from the third pillar
of Mount Dana
perhaps zippering
to the end

When news
came to me
in the mottled light
of the Valley Sequoia
and Incense Cedars

I didn't know
your death
and Ruby-crowned kinglet call
would go on and on with me
into the years

That every Christmas Bird Count
every peregrine fledging
from some wild eyrie
would make me think
of you.

IRREVERENT YOU
    —For Fred Beckey—climb on.

We met
in some bright lit hall
in Canada

Room full of people,
not one talking to you

Afraid of your enthusiastic voice
in the loud room

Projecting, because you can hardly hear
but talk, so ready to talk—

Sitting with you, keeper watching,
Yosemite on our lips

Long, hot Sierra Range
on our minds, on our hands

We talk of pitches and peaks—

And the good fortune that led us
to sleep in the rock pockets of crags.

Fred Beckey, renown American climber and mountaineering author, chose his own path outside of industry and "good manners" to embrace his passion for mountains and do what he loved: climb.

INNER GORGE

What did we find
in the Inner Gorge
the day we tied in;
rapped down wet ropes
over ledges
that left us blind to each other,
deaf to each other?

What did we learn
when we tested
the old anchors,
made it to the pool
full of myth fish
and lost souls,
pulled our gear
swam across—

To stand on a boulder
seeing only walls
and opportunity.

What old self
did we leave
in that deep place?

What new self
did we take away?

Taft Point and Cathedral Spires

Climbing Cathedral Spires

West of the meadow clouds rise
over sleeping black oaks
pines silver with rain

Drop by drop these old spires
and the weathered cathedral
carved from tenacity by water and wind

Granite full of cracks
routes of run out lines
all chossy and crumbling

Yet—lazing about
dormant Mariposa lily and wild iris bulbs
we dream of ascents still to be made.

Overdue to Synder and Killion Parson's Lodge Reading

In the "high and the wild"
we raced
to seek and see

Finish in time
to hear words
in the old stone cabin

Hear the rattle
of voices
across the wide meadow

While the sky
painted every dome
in light until the stars came

But we missed it—
too long on the rock
too slow on the hand break

even still—
tinged with forlorn desire
it was the best reason for being too late.

What You Leave Behind When You Jump
—For Sean "Stanley" Leary and Dean Potter

What you leave behind when you jump
is the fear;
whisked away by the whirling whipping wind
the stretch and pull of skin, the flapping, rapping
world going by. All the sound flooding
all the rocks careening, and you fly
with a wild roar.

What you leave behind when you jump
are the constraints;
of what you think and they think,
the dynamics of physics and thought,
all the commentary, the scoping, planning,
packing. All the moments of your heart
nearly exploding, your courage soaring
spirit glowing, you illuminate the sky
through your pores.

What you leave behind when you jump
is the past;
as you push yourself forward
forward pushing the line between the dance,
calling the moves between devil and dare, here and there
even the angels scream in ecstasy and disbelief
as you push higher.

What you leave behind when you jump
are the friends who counted down the launch for you,
the people waiting at the top, at the bottom, the cold beers
and warm smiles, the endless trail miles that have worn out your shoes.

What you leave behind when you jump
is your life
as you've known it;
the hands that held you, the friends that stood beside you,
the family that can never fill the void that was left
when you traded your parachute for magnificent wings;
once unfolded their raven blackness turned purple;
left this world in a wake of swirling turbulence;
your caw-call echoes on forever as you ascend from the BASE.

BASE jumping is the act of jumping without a tether, only a parachute from features such as a Bridge, Antenna, Span, or Earth.

NORTH DOME HUDDLE

Lightning pose
crouched and waiting
as the tantrum
of afternoon storms pass

Hazards everywhere
as the rain sheets down
granite slick and anything
upright attracts the light

So we hide
spread among pockets
of trees and boulders
singing

Songs rising
in the afternoon warmth
as the rain puddles
as the wind sweeps
our songs away

Summit

There is a smell rising, igneous gone white
molten rock cooled to granite, its flecked skin
full of tiny realms; worlds when heaped
make mountains.

Thin, the skin of our lives abrades easily
against its rough face, we cradle it anyway—
each subtle feature in the hand
of its admirer.

Balance the world as we may, friction
twist on toe, finger in small cracks
we move through this life like we do
on rock.

Navigate one crux at a time
until we can see beyond
every featured challenge
each blank space

Turn our myopic eyes to the summit wide world
to see everything, we could not imagine
laid so carefully across the Earth

Though, somehow—
we always sensed it was there.

ROCK WORK
   —Dedicated to all the Trail Crews

Paw path
Foot path
Horse trail
Wagon road

Rock work to hold the site

Every route, they say,
is a signature line.

Moonbow Mission

We come
to see the light
in the darkness

How the angle
of the full moon
reaching over rock

Its' touch
on mist in spring
high country winter runoff

Meltwater
turns ghost and spray
leaping to us

We catch it
in marveled eyes, on film
and mostly in the basins
of our very free spirits.

WHEN THE SUN RISES IN AUGUST, MONO LAKE

Tall beige stacks
of salt and brine, calcium heaps
up against wind and heat

We walk, sage scent and "lost"
not lost, in some other world

Gulls loud
sweeping apricot sky
thin whisp of cloud
light caught in the morning

A silent world
until birds perch
crack the cool air
with beckoning and boundaries

letting the desert heat creep in
letting the dry, dry heat creep in

TPR: Tioga Pass Resort
—For Jennifer and Henny

How many miles
ended for so many
on the stools of that lodge

Perched nearly 10,000 feet high
for over a hundred years
its back broken in the last big winter

But love
is a tireless thing

Each splintered log repaired
every collapse and rupture shored up
until the whole thing stood again

One day, soon
filled with everyone
sitting inside

The grime of every peak
and meadow, swept into a pile
at the end of the day

THE EARLY DAYS

Naked
leap into lake
shattered reflection
of crags and shaky spires

We run
light over the alpine
skin like braille
from the bugs biting

Race
through thin air
into a tiny blue tent
share ourselves for hours

In the middle of nowhere
for us
the center of everything

Jeffrey Pine Lined

Sweet warmth
caramel scent rising
this long trail
lined in butterscotch dreams

Pulsed by small cool breezes

Is just right
never a complaint
of how far the miles are
to where we are going

Trail Crew Prank

After dinner, camp chairs filled
with the ache of miles and heaved rocks,
we settle in for a lesson or some fireside tale.

They send me for a pen
carefully placed in the library
tucked neatly into a bear box.

Opening the cap
SHOCKED—some loud POP!
They all laugh.

How many times a summer
will they belly roll like that?

HIGH ANGLE RESCUE

When the wind howls
or the rocks come loose

slip of fingers in the crack
or friction gone slack

perhaps the rope catches
or the anchor holds

maybe there is no rope
at all

so when the bone shatters
or a finger pops off

when a partner calls
or another party steps up to step in

there are only a few
skilled enough to finish the job

bringing high climbing spirits
back to the grounding Earth.

FISHERMAN'S TRAIL

Always another way
the fisherman's trail
takes you direct
straight to the alpine lake

So your day
is spent lakeside
napping on granite
ready to see stars.

Leave the long miles
to the meandering trail
your strong calves
will get you there

And your hands
across one solid crux move
to arrive.

Eastern Sierra in Fall

OH! RIDGE

Freezing nights turn hot at day break
when the sun crests the ridge
pours light into our camp

Water locked tight in frozen patterns
eases back into its fluid self
and our muscles ease too—

Present, chill prick alive, sun warming
dart of Kinglets, a Golden-mantled squirrel
quick to work

Long exhale—
gift of this life to the next
gone out of me

into the Eastside juniper and sage.

Sugar Pine On The Ridge

I stand
with arthritic branches
aged by snow, topped by lightning
malformed by wind, and to the ridge
I am protection from
such forces.

She is
not far from me
a record of winters
and springs I have not seen.
Steadfast against the storms
the biting forces, she is tired—
more tired than I, and worn,
scoured with half shed limbs,
and barely any needles.
Today, still, she stands
not far from me
my mother.

THE ALCHEMY OF WOOD

Board feet, stiff and steady
before the aged decline and drying,
joints fitted, hold taut, bear weight.

In the sun the wood breaths.
In the wind it exhales.
In the cold it holds its breath,
the cells of it sit still.

Year after year it stands
takes the bumps, earns nicks
cracks when the earth shifts,
wishes it could shoo away
the rodents.

One day, it crumples
into a heap of decay
or lump of char.

I find, I worked too hard, bucked
large trees who collapsed in storms
piled their crowns and lit them
so the day could see their glory
and the night could not forget them.

I patted their root ball holes level
after heaving good soil and wildcrafting
flower seeds into them.

I sat on their broken bodies
exhausted. Trunks older than I or anyone
I've known. I reveled in their once starry views,
their long stoic stand.

Today, I find their alchemy has seized me.
Muscles, appendages turned wood,
joints bear weight and do not bend.
Line by line, I am marking
my winters and my summers
as they always have.
One day, I too
will be ash.

"Oak Tree, Snowstorm"

They say
a famous photo
was taken here,
but the ermine who rents
the hollow oak branch
that fell last year
and hides the spot
pays no mind
to human
history.

Ansel Adams photographed a prominent Oak Tree in Yosemite Valley and the image is titled "Oak Tree, Snowstorm."

LESSONS FROM THE EAST

Cool air on naked skin
meanders in, enters
from the East, signals
relief from a wicked
summer.

The oaks, Valley, Black, Blue,
feel beat up after the hot
dry season that is ebbing.
They drop their leaves
or they don't.

Even after a harrowing
summer, where a sneeze
could catch the forest
on fire, it is hard to look
away, hard to leave.

In its quietness, solitude
is found; in its old trees
stability and fortitude
are taught; in its patience
with storms, we learn how
to weather the catastrophic
drought.

The deeply rooted forest
is endlessly teaching us
lessons from the East.

WAWONA

Blue-black night and platinum moon
full and glowing, circle—thin ring of moisture
gives hint at a coming rain

Washed in silver light, quiet steps
across the meadow an owl chatters
to me and we raise our voices together

One call back and forth
to show, even in darkness
we can find each other.

WOODBURNING

Almond
from the Central Valley
has turned to ash
primed by pine
finished by oak.

That is how
the house is warmed
after harvest season
after brutal storms
lay down the tired trees.

On The Stairs of Old Galen's Cabin, New Year's Day

Quiet
among snow
and draped sunlight

Through
the canopy
of reaching trees

She comes
a tiny weasel
her coat gone ermine

Camouflage
among snowdrifts and banks
among tree wells and hidden places

She is curious to know
her dark eyes sparking
between her twitchy stance

*What
have you found?
What are you doing?*

*Sitting here
so still, so quiet
just being.*

Sitting here
so still, so quiet
just being.

Navigation Point

You'll find it.
Mountain heather
alpine meadow hardy
framed in talus;
a day's walk
from the glacier.

El Capitan Night Sky

The Dawn Wall By Night

Footsteps crushing leaves
scent of bay rising
disturbance of duff and shrub

Up the drainage, boulder dance
prusik on a fixed line
pulling up high enough

Above the chaos
to see the mission
clearly

Sun sets, rose light gone—
from the ledge you see
the lights come on

Careful watch, hear the heaving
gravity in its finest form
testing people

This generous winter, vision rising,
it goes, is freed and history is made
on the Dawn Wall

June Lake Rituals: Leaf Peeping

Meandering
soft as the flows of our late summer creek
of the rivers, turn by turn, slowed by the heat
now sleepy in the cold
they grace us

This time each year
wander among us, carry out their own rituals
what beauty they bring, what joy, in the vast array
of their magnificent faces
as they revel at us

Us, shimmering aspens
our gold-red banners unrolled
in the first breezes of fall, we shutter in the early chill
they delight; their warm hands on our parchment trunks
to say, we are kin

Do they know
how we long for their return
all the other seasons
of the year?

A Man Name William

I found you
set beneath a granite flake
on the top of Fresno Dome.
Certainly, you had not
been there long, surely
I would have noticed
you before.

But today, on a crisp fall morning
the breeze touching all the tree tops
and the view nearly clear to the coast

I found you, a heap of ash
left on the peak
in a plastic bag
a small plastic label
and round tin tag
the only hints
of your story.

I left you there
questioning if it was right
to leave you in the bag
which had already been
bitten and torn open—
perhaps it would have been better
to raise you up
and let you fly
into the great wilderness

With people summiting
it wasn't my place;
nothing about it
seemed right.

This is what I know,
what I recall—
your name is William
and your ashes are more
then ten years old,
someone had been holding on to you.
You were cremated
close to my own home
and somehow
it is a small world,
proven, again.

Time has passed
I have thought of you often,
during the wind
the rain, the first snow
all the visitors
to that peak.

Are you still there?
Easing your way out of the bag
into the wild?

I went back for you.

Braving the icy road
pedaling the grade.
If you were there
I would set you free
speak some gentle words
let you go into the world
free of your life,
free of your body, free from the bag
into the cycle of the universe.

If you were gone
you were gone.

The chill was biting until the grade warmed me
and I started up the trail, to the talus;
finally, walking the wet
decomposing granite to the top.

I was excited to see you
not knowing if you would be there.

I searched and for a moment,
I thought you might be gone—
yet, there tucked beneath the flake
your gray-white ash spilling out
you remained.

Part of you to the youngest Jeffrey pine
on the dome, the bravest tree
set with the grandest view
its lifetime of centuries still before it

You hardy its stance,
nourish its roots.
The rest of you set gently on the wind
your dust matching the rock;
You are the mountain now—
nothing between you and her enduring flesh.

Set free from your life
set free from your body
set free from your bag.
Rooted in the mountain
enduring in the wilderness.
A man name William
I never knew, yet set you free
on a mountain high in November.
Your placard I could not find
so I know nothing more
than what I remember and have only
your cremation tag as any final proof
you were there.

Risk And Resolve

FIRE SEASON

Parched as bleached bones
the stale grass stands stiff.
The sun sucks everything
drier and drier, even the Earth
cracks and crumbles.

The tips of the fresh growth
on all the forest trees, turns, burns
its new flesh no match for wicked heat
that kills off the growth
sends even the eldest trees
into stress.

Manzanitas with adaptations
are no better off, their round
green gray leaves yellow
while their berries fall wrinkled
wasted in the desiccating air.

The mountainside tartan
woven of pine, oak, grasses and shrubs
recoils in the rising waves of heat
day after day, succumbing to the drawdown
of moisture lost every moment
the sun shines.

Roses crisp on the vine;
iris bloom then burn;
vetch, buttercups, peas
reveal their faces then coil up
incensed at the violation.
Wildflowers attempt a momentary
song, then disappear.

While the hands of men, women and children
cut, clip, rake, haul,
trim all the bits of nature that spring up
around them, create a break, carve out
safe space and a little hope.
Blisters, cuts, splitters, rash,
a spreading itch, dirt caked faces;
nostrils when blown, leave tissue paper
black.

Only the dirt comes off in the shower,
that doesn't calm the fear, cleanse the ache
refresh the ground, heal the parched world

This year, this drought, its long grip still tight,
will kill nearly half the forest, and one can only wonder
what the stench of its mortality will be—

that of veins which pump no more, run dry,
barely decay in the lack of moisture and relentless heat—
or will all be swallowed in smoke and indiscriminate flames

in a roiling storm that defies physics,
makes its own weather and sends all of us running
this fire season.

SIFTERS

Indeed, dear California
it has come to this
a stack of sifters
a pair of gloves

To find
what has burned
what is lost
after the fire cools.

Fire In The Canyon

Heat
up out of the canyon
flowers pushed skyward
Redbuds popping against blue sky
spring river rush
runs

Sunlit
Poppy coyness
left behind when the blossom
sheath fell, open to the air
to the light, you turn the canyon
to flower fire

Every
rolling hill ablaze
same brilliant orange
that scorched this Earth
last fall, and again, no one
can look away.

Sequoia Groves

Encroachment from all sides
fire on the edges
ash in the air
duff deprived by drought

What will it take
to save what is sacred,
letting life live
long beyond our own years?

ENDANGERED
   —Dedicated to all who have worked to save and protect the Pacific Fisher.

When the trees fell
and the once lively forest
came quiet

When the small creeks
plumbed for water
irrigated weed

And cars crossed topo lines
between passes, along rivers
making everything harder to cross

the fishers started to disappear.

Their lineages born
inside the hallows of big trees
life girth hitched to the wide and reaching

Natal dens in fire scars
or trees once touched by lightning
snapped tops broken by wind

Middle cousin of wolverine, of marten
you lost lives to fur traps, expansion
the slow cuts of creep and drug lords

A pocket of you survived anyway.

You, so unknown, go on
your darting hunting ways
quick and quiet

Among woods
among pines, cedars, Sequoias
broken Bear clover and wafts of musk

Your flashes
between tangled timbers
and overgrowth

Hidden high above our heads
filling hallow spaces
you go on—

Sparking life
eyes and ears closed, tiny
young kits, who soon

will rise from their airborne dens
to look out at the forest
that remains.

Halt of The Lyell

You have stopped moving
since they staked you out
so many years ago.

Rambled your edges
peeked beneath the undercuts of ice
slipped on loose talus.

Nestled north facing between crags
drought years again and again
melt water stealing your crown

No longer able to slide under the weight
of your glistening adornments
today they call you an ice field.

In 2012 the Lyell Glacier, once Yosemite's largest glacier, was found to no longer be moving—the key characteristic that defines a glacier. The Lyell Glacier along with the McClure Glacier were originally recorded and studied by John Muir in the late 1800's.

The High Country

Rock backbone serves you well
through the millennia of your becoming
through the days of our own undoing

When we have wiped the natural systems
free of their function, when we have distorted
their will—to focus on recovery instead of thrive

We have bent their kind ways
to our temperamental whims, then turn our backs—
your backbone of igneous, feldspar, quartz

Will weather the temporary occupation of us
will go on and on beyond timeframes
we can dream

While those of us who are so endeared
to your rounded domes, your eroded ridges
will long, through the realms, to be there with you.

YOSEMITE

You have no *voice*
though some can hear
exactly
what you are saying.

Paradigm Shift

Along the banks
fractured trees in thousands
of pieces, strewn across meadows
hung up on each other
windstorm or reckoning

Heaps of woody debris
burn piles, timber temples
that cannot be lit
everything too dry
everything too filled
with risk

Even as the life
is sucked out of this place
soil turned to sand
forest turned to charcoal
the Sugar Pines remember
the good days

Fire off some butterscotch scent
trigger memory across the air
woo us out of sleep
so we remember too—
woo us, to the work
the stewardship that repairs
what we alone have done

CRUSHING THE DRY SEASON

Each flake bends its trajectory
towards the glass, splatters
its icy innards on the windshield.

Up and down the drainage
tree branches accentuated
two-tone, white on wet bark
they stand guard over the icy highway.

In the darkness, edge of asphalt
a buck sways his head,
tilts his heavy rack
to look through the storm

parts the snowflakes to see.
Power twist on hooves, he turns
darts down the slope
away from the road.

Everything is wet,
everything is cold,
in the first real storm
of winter.

Finally here—
crushing the dry season
making summer too
turn tail and run.

RECONCILE

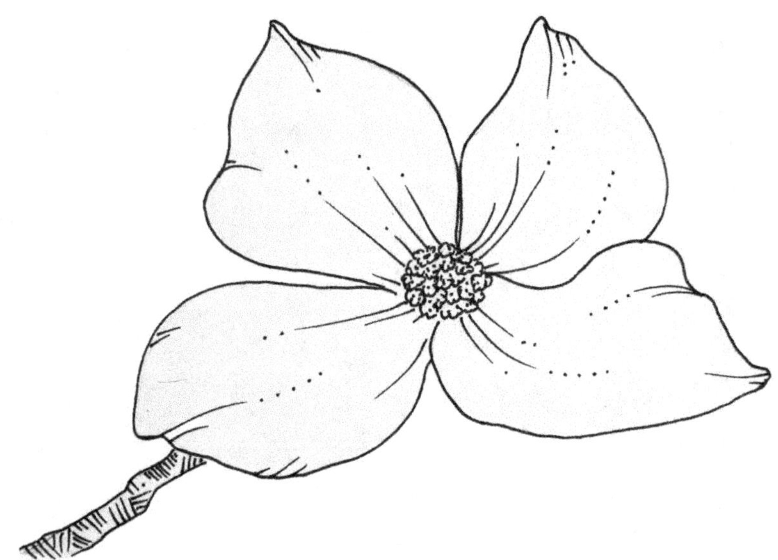

SODA SPRINGS

Even in this darkness
where quiet is not lonesome,
but simply a coming to rest

I can hear your uprising
in the dark, that effervescent essence
floating up through unseen channels

of granite, soil, bacteria, fungi
pushing up and breaking through

wet bubbles that burst with giving
whose seamless forms cannot contain
the excitement of gas or spirit

that must break free
at the surface—that gives up everything
to become air and sky.

SIGNMAKER
    —For Les

More than direction
you centered us: generous greetings
then guide

How many souls
have you put on the right path
all the miles, all the journey steps

 of our days on Earth.

SIERRA LOVE POEM

Scars of dogwood blossoms
twisted scarlet snow plants
still the aura of the rising Sierra
hangs in all my cells—how easily
I can recall the piney Earth
her sibling-scent, even now
from two thousand
thirty-three miles
away.

Scents of Place

Can you know a place
by the scent that rises
in the morning, in a season?

Can you know
just where you are
in a large, expanding world?

Triangulate yourself
between the tang-sweet scent
of Bear clover and Jeffery pine

the woody duff warmed by sun.
If you do, I will know
right where you are.

Unsettled Watch

A finch nestles
into the platform
of the motion light
that points
at the front door.

Each night, with the days
so cold and short
it settles in, fills its down
with air, trapped warmth
against the chill.

All these months
have given us time
to know each other,
reveal our patterns
live side by side.

The bird never stirs
when we emerge or
return. It watches us
or sleeps, knowing
it is safe on our threshold.

A few days ago,
we found
a mound of feathers
a blood stain,
we watched and fretted—

That is the way, when love
nests in your heart.
At dusk, our small bird
returned, sits, even now,
undisturbed. Its head tucked
deep into its wing, sleeping.

Blossom Trail Weakness

Imagine the view
those wild geese must have
when they leave the wetlands,
vernal pools reserved for them

Flying over acres and acres
of perfectly square orchards
erupting in raucous blooms
their scent luring every bee for miles

Do they delight
in the strict rows of pink and fragrance
five petal white blush blossoms
that soon will be fruit?

So much nature
has been cut and carved
out of this place—and still
it is hard to not fall fancy

to the Blossom Trail.
Try!—Try not to kiss your lover
while standing under those
luscious trees

while the wild poppies
orange, and catching
delight in your weakness!

SUNRISE IN CAMP

Morning sun on my face
brush through knots
of matted hair
I am a mess
and perfectly happy.

Beyond Ghosts and Gods

I want to know
the tenacious flower
that pushes
against gravity

Blooms
face skyward
or reverent
to the Earth

On what are believed
unforgiving crags
harboring only
ghosts and gods.

YEARS LATER
   —For Chris

We walk
among Black oaks gone gold
along low rivers, tired from summer

Pay respects
at the stumps of fallen trees
taken down by high winds or lightning

While calling up
memories of years
and youths gone by.

We untie
the drawstring of some old bag
dig around in its clanking contents

Find a bottle
of champaign, attempt a quiet uncork
in the sound shower of the Falls.

This is for you
my good friend, teacher of so many
and the years we both continue to savor.

EPHEMERAL

Water down the narrow creek
disappears under the covered bridge
so many lively spirits walked this world
leaf on water, pine needle in duff

Boot strike
mule hoof
stagecoach horse
all of it crossing the bridge

Time on, again and again, it goes—
while we blow away
into nothing but stories
and
    thin
        fleeting
            whisps
                of

                    m e m o r y .

YOSEMITE DAWNING

I know where the sun comes up
crests the edge of Half Dome
on my birthday—late summer.
We go, each year,
watch the light rise.

You have never failed me
by my side at that early hour
eager as our eyes to the dawn,
to the fractured night
when the light comes.

Nothing has ever held us back
crisp air, light coat of ice
on black road, snapping
timber of Mono winds
catastrophic fire.

Nothing has held us back
from the new day: tiny,
quiet celebrations only we know
huddled together, warmed
by ourselves held close.

Breath and step, dream or ache,
inseparable. Year after year
snow storm or summer heat, unwavering.
We savor it, this connection we have—
watching Yosemite dawning.

Now I know, the sun will always rise
crest the ridge of Half Dome
on my birthday in just the same place
into millennia—pouring light
into the Valley as it does now

even with you gone—
my old, good dog.

Someday, my birthday will be ink
alongside my death and all that will matter
is that the light still comes

and I hope
someone is there to watch
Yosemite dawning.

Shauna Potocky and Roo at Glacier Point watching a birthday sunrise, 2016

Author's Note

When I originally wrote the piece that *So Signed, Lincoln* was adapted from, I did not fully understand the complexities and challenges associated with the founding of our country, including the establishment of public lands. As I reflect on that piece today, it is a reminder of the critical importance of telling and teaching the whole story. That public lands have deep histories. These places have as much to teach us about humanity and our society as they do their wonder and reason for establishment.

This is an invitation to learn more about the areas you are connected to.

Ask yourself, whose homeland? Learn the deep history of where you live and the places you visit and love.

The last remaining intact landscapes and seascapes are in our hands, it is a vital reminder that we all must be stewards.

There have always been challenges
they have always been faced
and we are in awe
of the overcoming

Our inheritance gifted us this moment
daunting as it may feel, there is hope
in our doing, in the awe
of our own overcoming

ACKNOWLEDGMENTS

Thank you to all the people who have inspired me to write throughout the years. To Linda Wolvek, one of my earliest literature teachers who was patient and encouraging. To University of Santa Cruz, Professor Emeritus John Dizikus, who was the first person to review an early draft of my collected poetry, nearly a decade after having been his student and years before this book of poetry came into being. I had hoped to share this book with you.

Thank you to the *"Tuesday Night Tellers"* Parker Kimball, Grant Kniefel, Jessica Ramsey Golden, Carey Seward, and Kyle Walker for the power of our consistent practice, and the depth of our support and collaborations. To Marcia Meirer for your thoughtful guidance, open heart and support organizing my entire collection of work. I am so grateful.

To the remarkable people that make up the communities of Yosemite, California and Seward, Alaska. It is the deep care, connection and support of each other's dreams that allow projects such as this to be birthed into the world. Your influence in my life is impossible to measure. I am so grateful to you.

Thank you to Sandra Kleven, Michael Burwell and Signe Nichols of Cirque Press. I am forever touched by your passion for writing and the arts, for your deep love of *Cirque Journal*, Cirque Press, Poetry Parley and every other thing you touch that turns to magic. The depth of our connection, the insight gained in our conversations and the opportunities that bloom from your effort, brighten the world for all of us. I am humbled to be among your published authors.

To the amazing Penny Otwell, whose paintings and art I have admired for years. You have helped make a dream come true and I, again and again, am so grateful for your generosity in gracing this book with your outstanding expressions of Yosemite, which we both love so deeply.

Colby Brokvist, world class guide, naturalist and photographer—thank you for the incredible eye you had for catching that moment at Duey Point. Magic! Your influence in my life is substantial and does not go unnoticed.

Kirk Keeler, thank you for capturing the essence of my spirit in so many photographs and allowing this book to feature a genuine moment of awe. I know, you know, Sequoias are my kin.

"What You Leave Behind When You Jump" was published by *Alaska Women Speak: Ghosts and Spirits*, Fall 2018, Volume 26, Issue 3.

"The Alchemy of Wood" was published by *Alaska Women Speak: Stoking The Fire*, Winter 2018, Volume 26, Issue 4.

"Yosemite Dawning" was published by *Beyond Words International Literary Magazine*, September 2021.

About the Author

Photo by Kirk Keeler

Shauna Potocky has a deep love of jagged peaks, rough edged ridgelines, ice and natural ecosystems, where the wonder of the world unfolds, teaches and continuously holds mystery and awe. Shauna spent her childhood in the San Fernando Valley of Los Angeles, California living in an urban landscape framed by dry creek beds and scrub filled hills.

It was the Sierra Nevada that showed her, if you take time to quiet the external pressures and focus on discovering who you are—you can find yourself. You can find joy in carefully packing a bag to go out—to walk for miles, to strain against gravity and your thoughts, go light into the granite, into the realms of seldom seen wildflowers, marmot lookouts, and peak scraping sunrises. You can go far beyond the limits society sets for us and focus on the person you want to be and become. And, as many say, the wildlife don't care what you wear.

Shauna learned to love, to be a steward, and what respect and humility are. That joy is as simple as having just what you need, a journal, a few remarkable people to share it with and a good dog. A very good dog.

Along the way, she was mentored, guided and taught to value and care for wild places. That lives depend on these remarkable landscapes and seascapes—and that more lives will need them tomorrow. For livelihood, for joy or for both. Shauna works towards that every day.

Shauna is a poet and painter, who lives in Seward, Alaska located within the traditional homelands of the Sugpiaq people.

About the Artist—Penny Otwell

Photo by Richard Beebe

Yosemite visitors are often deeply moved by their first glimpse of this unique glacially carved valley and some even shake their heads in disbelief when they first see it. The awe and wonder of why Yosemite deeply touches all of us is why painter, Penny Otwell paints Yosemite.

Otwell arrived in 1964 and worked for The Ahwahnee Hotel, but her newfound love of hiking and backpacking out of Tuolumne Meadows captured her heart. She was hooked! And this passion for being in wild places directly influenced her to become a painter. The self-taught artist makes drawings, some watercolors, but oil painting is her prime medium that collectors recognize in her signature style.

All paintings begin on a portable easel "en plein air." The artist and the landscape make a strong visual design connection resulting in the abstraction of the scene that also includes a certain sense of reality. Some pieces are completed outdoors, but there is often a hard critique in the studio before the painting is ever shown in a gallery.

Otwell says, "My interest in oil paint is in the paint itself. It's like sculpture in the way I use a palette knife, building up impasto paint passages to depict Sierra rock formations. My use of color originates from the way I feel about the landscape and wanting to share this with others. I want you to see the brush and knife strokes that mimic Yosemite's magnificent geological arrangements. After all, paint is like soil and sand that my palette knife moves and shapes into intriguing designs."

—Penny Otwell, 2022

About Cirque Press

Cirque Press grew out of *Cirque*, a literary journal that publishes the works of writers and artists from the North Pacific Rim, a region that reaches north from Oregon to the Yukon Territory, south through Alaska to Hawaii, and west to the Russian Far East.

Cirque Press is a partnership of Sandra Kleven, publisher, and Michael Burwell, editor. Ten years ago, we recognized that works of talented writers in the region were going unpublished, and the Press was launched to bring those works to fruition. We publish fiction, nonfiction, and poetry, and we seek to produce art that provides a deeper understanding about the region and its cultures. The writing of our authors is significant, personal, and strong.

Sandra Kleven — Michael Burwell, publishers and editors

www.cirquejournal.com

BOOKS FROM CIRQUE PRESS

Apportioning the Light by Karen Tschannen (2018)

The Lure of Impermanence by Carey Taylor (2018)

Echolocation by Kristin Berger (2018)

Like Painted Kites & Collected Works by Clifton Bates (2019)

Athabaskan Fractal: Poems of the Far North by Karla Linn Merrifield (2019)

Holy Ghost Town by Tim Sherry (2019)

Drunk on Love: Twelve Stories to Savor Responsibly by Kerry Dean Feldman (2019)

Wide Open Eyes: Surfacing from Vietnam by Paul Kirk Haeder (2020)

Silty Water People by Vivian Faith Prescott (2020)

Life Revised by Leah Stenson (2020)

Oasis Earth: Planet in Peril by Rick Steiner (2020)

The Way to Gaamaak Cove by Doug Pope (2020)

Loggers Don't Make Love by Dave Rowan (2020)

The Dream That Is Childhood by Sandra Wassilie (2020)

Seward Soundboard by Sean Ulman (2020)

The Fox Boy by Gretchen Brinck (2021)

Lily Is Leaving: Poems by Leslie Ann Fried (2021)

One Headlight by Matt Caprioli (2021)

November Reconsidered by Marc Janssen (2021)

Callie Comes of Age by Dale Champlin (2021)

Someday I'll Miss This Place Too by Dan Branch (2021)

Out There In The Out There by Jerry McDonnell (2021)

Fish the Dead Water Hard by Eric Heyne (2021)

Salt & Roses by Buffy McKay (2022)

Growing Older In This Place:
   A Life in Alaska's Rainforest by Margo Wasserman Waring (2022)

Kettle Dance: A Big Sky Murder by Kerry Dean Feldman (2022)

Nothing Got Broke by Larry F. Slonaker (2022)

On the Beach: Poems 2016-2021 by Alan Weltzien (2022)

Sky Changes on the Kuskokwim by Clifton Bates (2022)

Transplanted: A Memoir by Birgit Lennertz Sarrimanolis (2022)

Between Promise and Sadness by Joanne Townsend (2022)

The Sky, The Ocean, The Stars by Scott Hanson (2023)

Yosemite Dawning by Shauna Potocky (2023)

CIRCLES — Illustrated books from Cirque Press

Baby Abe: A Lullaby for Lincoln by Ann Chandonnet (2021)

Miss Tami, Is Today Tomorrow? by Tami Phelps (2021)

Miss Bebe Goes to America by Lynda Humphrey (2022)

Rock Sanctuary by Penny Otwell

REFLECTIONS ON YOSEMITE DAWNING

Yosemite Dawning by Shauna Potocky is a beautiful collection of poems that honors the earth and the land. These are poems that celebrate the ways in which nature reveals its beauty and wonders to those who observe carefully. Her words and language are prayers and hymns to the mysteries that too many of us miss or take for granted in our day to day lives, revealing the existence of natural phenomena that infuse our world with mystery and beauty. Her words allow us to witness the transformation that can take place when we are thoughtful stewards of the natural world, when we are alive to everything that surrounds us outdoors.

—Patricia A. Smith, author of *The Year of Needy Girls*